101 WAYS TO HELP THE PLANET

A One Year Challenge

Make One Small Change a Week to Help the Environment

Gaia Appello

101 Ways to Help the Planet

ISBN: 978-0-9956710-2-7

CONTENTS

Feel Good - Do Good

Become an Environment Hero!

Make One Change a Week to Help the Environment

Welcome to 101 Ways to Help the Planet - a one-year challenge that will help you build environmentally friendly habits into your life week by week. This book invites you to try something new that helps the planet each week for a year. The challenges are designed to fit in with your life and your budget. This way you can make changes bit by bit without becoming overwhelmed.

I was inspired to create this book by the amazing story of Afroz Shah, a lawyer from Mumbai who was shocked by the vast amount of rubbish that had washed up on his childhood beach. Together with a neighbour, he headed out and started collecting rubbish. The beach was knee deep in rubbish in some places and the task for two people seemed just impossible, but Afroz led by example. He inspired and encouraged others, and soon larger and larger groups of volunteers joined him to help him clean the beach. Afroz was awarded the Champion of the Earth award by the UN in 2016 and has inspired a worldwide movement for people to clean up their local environment. Today Versova beach is again beautiful and turtles have returned to nest there. The task of improving the environment can seem overwhelming, but we can all take small steps to help in our own homes and neighbourhoods. The more people take up the challenge, the more these small acts add up to create a big change. *

How to use this book

At the beginning of this book you will find a list of 101 different weekly challenges. Each week choose a challenge from the list to have a go at. There is also space for you to write in your own challenges and ideas. When you try a challenge, do your best to complete it for the week. At the end of the week, look back and see how it went. If it went really well, you can keep it up for the rest of the month, or forever! If it didn't work out for you, write down what wasn't working and just move on to the next challenge. At the end of every four weeks there is space to reflect on how the challenges are going. There are a wide range of suggestions to choose from, with challenges at different levels, and some are more long term than others. Swapping one brand of shampoo for another may be an easily achievable challenge, but growing your own strawberries will take several months. Choose suggestions at a level you are comfortable with, or be inspired and come up with your own ideas.

Here are some tips for making it work:

1. Look through the list and see if you do any of these challenges already, if you do go ahead and tick them off and take a moment to feel great about the things that you are already doing.

2. Start small with some that you think you are highly likely to succeed at. Starting out with small achievable goals will help your success breed success.

3. If you try something and it doesn't work out, don't beat yourself up about it. Rate it as unlikely that you will keep it up and move on. It might be helpful to write a note about why it's not for you. Remember that it may not be the right time, and in the future you may be able to come back to it if circumstances are different.

4. If you miss a week don't worry, the weeks are not dated, just carry on from where you left off. You have completed the challenge when you have completed 52 weeks, they do not all need to be done in one calendar year.

5. Share your successes and swap tips and ideas with other people.

6. Remember you don't have to stick with our challenges, create your own, ask friends or family, get the kids involved in thinking of ideas, or have a look around the many online groups and forums where people are sharing ideas every day.

At the end of the year there is space to reflect on how it has gone overall. Ask yourself how much of an impact have your changes had when they are all added up? We think you will be surprised and pleased!

Remember, this challenge is all about making positive changes in a positive way - it is not here to make you feel bad about yourself. If you find yourself failing at challenges, try finding projects or changes that look as though they will fit in very well with your life. If you fail several in a row, that's ok, take a moment to think about why they are not working out and use this to guide you to challenges that are more likely to stick. We are all living with our own backpack of life circumstances. Meet yourself where you are and move forwards from there. Remember, your small changes will add up over time.

Taking the first step on any journey is often the hardest. You have already done that by buying this book, so let's put one foot after the other and see where this adventure takes us!

*If you are interested in the inspirational story of Afroz Shah you can see the huge transformation on Versova beach on YouTube

101 Ways to Help the Planet

101 Challenges

Here we have suggested 101 ideas for ways you can make a change that will help to add up to a big change for the environment. Choose a different challenge to try each week, or make up your own using these as inspiration. Go through the list and tick off any you already do, then choose a challenge you feel fairly confident you can succeed at to start off your first week.

No	✓	Challenge
1		Check the back of your fridge and give it a clean this week. Lots of dust and dirt on the coils can cause it to use more electricity to cool your food, a clean may help save electricity and money, especially if you have pets.
2		This week organise and commit to using reusable drinks containers, including water bottles and coffee cups.
3		Commit to buying as much organic food as you can for one week. Did you notice any difference? Are there any organic items that you could consider swapping long term?
4		Swap sandwich bags and food wrap for reusable food containers and beeswax wraps where possible. You can even make your own beeswax wraps with cotton fabric and beeswax pellets in the oven – maybe also make some for friends and family as gifts!
5		This week help keep local knowledge and traditions alive while helping the environment. How did people in your local area live two, three or even four generations ago? How did they overcome everyday challenges? Is there an 'old way' of doing things that may be more ecologically friendly than the new? Or perhaps there is a recipe made of local seasonal ingredients that can be revived?
6		If you have a garden or patio, try growing your own fruits and vegetables. You don't need to dig the entire garden over, start small with some tomatoes in a pot, some strawberries and runner beans and see how you go. You can grow potatoes in a special sack, they are easy to care for and harvest.
7		Use vinegar to get rid of limescale in your home instead of harsh chemicals. Soak the item in vinegar (or a vinegar water mix) or if it is a tap or other hard to reach area put a cloth soaked in vinegar over it and leave for a few hours before wiping clean.

No	✓	Challenge
8		Buy your next item of clothing fair trade. Look out for fair trade clothing brands who make it transparent how much people are getting paid and that the working conditions are good.
9		Keep your own chickens for happy eggs and fertilizer for the garden, or see if it is possible to find somewhere locally (farmers' market, farm shop or similar) that sells fresh eggs from well cared for chickens.
10		Swap 5 things in your weekly shop for a more local option.
11		Before buying anything this week ask yourself: Do I need it? Can I afford it? Can I make do another way?
12		This week set up a garden water butt. Mains tap water is high quality and has taken energy and resources to clean and deliver to our houses safe to drink, but plants don't need perfectly clean water to flourish. Collecting rainwater and storing it safely to use on your garden helps to preserve resources and reduces the amount that goes into the sewerage system. Make sure to clean water buts every year.
13		Join (or start) a given in kindness group in your area. This could be a facebook group, a community forum, or a message board in your local area.
14		Have a look around your home and think about how you could improve your insulation this week. Thick curtains and draft excluders can help reduce drafts and keep you warm, or if you only have single pane glass windows, you may want to look into using shrink fill window kits or other inexpensive secondary glazing options.
15		Buy recycled paper products - kitchen roll, toilet roll printer paper and more can all be bought recycled, check the label when you are shopping this week.
16		Double check what your local council will accept as recycling and where collection points are. Is there anything you can begin to recycle that you don't currently?
17		Reduce indoor air pollution by removing chemical air fresheners and plugins and using essential oils and plants that help purify the air, such as Aspidistra.

No	✓	Challenge
18		Make your own chemical free and plastic free deodorant using 50g organic cold pressed coconut oil, 85g bicarbonate of soda and 2 tablespoons of arrowroot powder. Melt the coconut oil over a low heat and stir in the other ingredients. Pour into clean jam jars or cosmetic pots and use a teaspoon or lollipop stick to scrape a little out when it has hardened. If it melts in warm weather, then give it a stir before using. Try it out, it really works!
19		Take your own sandwich or packed lunch into work this week instead of buying pre-packaged.
20		Walk or cycle somewhere this week instead of taking the car, or if that's not possible 'park and stride' parking some distance away and walking the last stretch.
21		Buy fruit and vegetables that are in season for one week. What was available? How did it go? Can you incorporate more seasonal fruit and veg into an ordinary week?
22		Think about your battery usage this week. Keep a box for used batteries and take them to a recycling point when full. Start using rechargeable batteries where you can.
23		Switch to online billing wherever you can. Most suppliers support this, and some even reward it.
24		Keep a note of how many hours you spent in the car this week. Can you reduce it anywhere?
25		Plant a herb garden, or grow some herbs in a window box. They take little care once established, you can enjoy fresh organic herbs and the bees and butterflies will love the flowers.
26		Create a wild patch in your garden. By encouraging insect life you are also encouraging the many different kinds of wildlife that feed on them.
27		Preserve something yourself this week - jam, chutney, freezing or canning.

No	✓	Challenge
28		Have a look in your food cupboard and check the labels of your favourite biscuits, chocolate spread, or other foods and looking to see if they use unsustainable palm oil (sustainable palm oil will have RSPO on the label). Write a letter or an email to at least one company and ask them to switch. Many won't make the change until their customers let them know how important it is to them.
29		Replace one plastic food storage container with glass this week.
30		Make your garden more bird friendly. Our gardens are now havens for wildlife including birds, even small changes will help. Certain bird populations are under pressure due to habitat loss and other environmental changes. See which birds are declining in your area and take action to make some changes to help. Put bird boxes up and provide water in a bird bath. You may also be able to plant shrubs and trees that provide cover and nesting opportunities for birds, or winter food such as berries.
31		If you need to regularly water your garden look into soaker hose or drip irrigation methods that can be more water efficient than your usual hosepipe (and save you time too). Timers, or smart irrigation controllers can make your system even more efficient.
32		Research an environmental issue and share your findings with two people.
33		Learn to love loose leaf tea and do away with tea bags. Individual infusers mean you do not have to make a large pot each time.
34		Ask an older relative or friend to share their make do and mend tips this week. If they tell you something good share it - don't let their knowledge fade away!
35		Buy or crochet lightweight reusable bags for buying loose vegetables instead of single use plastic bags.
36		Focus on helping your local wild bee populations – plant plenty of native flowering plants with a variety of shapes and sizes to accommodate different bees. Build bee hotels and leave some long grass where burrowing bees can nest. Garden organically so that bees are not harmed by pesticides.

No	✓	Challenge
37		Plant some butterfly friendly flowers in your garden, a window box or in pots. You can buy pollinator friendly seed mix, or check your local butterfly conservation society website for gardening ideas to help butterflies and moths.
38		Recycle old mobile phones. Many houses have a drawer with an old mobile or two stuffed in it. While you may want to keep an emergency spare, selling or recycling redundant mobile phones helps to save energy, conserve valuable metals that otherwise have to be mined, and stops hazardous materials ending up in landfill.
39		Try out a shampoo soap bar for one week and see if it works for you (best in soft water areas).
40		Bulk buying or shopping for loose and refillable products can save you money and reduce packaging waste. Long lasting staples like rice and pasta can be bought bulk but need to be stored correctly. Keep in mason jars or other reusable containers. It is also possible to get shampoo, conditioner, household cleaner, laundry liquid and similar refilled with environmentally friendly options such as Ecover using your own containers. See if there are any refill stations near where you live.
41		Start feeding the birds in your garden this week. Providing food all year round can really support your local bird population. Birds will eat lots of different foods, so as well as commercially available foods you can put out certain kitchen scraps such as plain cooked pasta and bread crusts. If cats are a problem in your area put the food high up on a table where cats can't reach, with a cone at the bottom to prevent climbing.
42		Create a nature highway in your garden. Ensure that small wildlife such as frogs, voles and other small visitors can move in and out of your garden. If it is tightly fenced in make a nature door at the bottom of your fence if safe to do so, or add a climbing plant to act like a ladder.
43		When buying clothes or other fabric items look out for hemp, linen, and wool. These are all natural textiles that have a low environmental impact.
44		Switch chargers off at the wall when not in use.

No	✓	Challenge
45		Start your own compost heap. Having a compost heap in your garden will help keep waste out of landfill, as well as providing organic fertiliser for your garden. If you have very little outdoor space, or only a balcony or patio you can still use a worm bin or compost tumbler for your kitchen scraps.
46		Try to buy loose fruit and vegetables where you can. If shops don't offer it, write a letter or email asking them to start.
47		Volunteer for a wildlife or environmental organisation locally.
48		How many household electrics are on standby at night? Can you switch them off?
49		Go organic in your garden. Help butterflies, insects and other wildlife by keeping your garden chemical free.
50		Replace chemical air fresheners in your home and your car with natural scents such as essential oils. Use bicarbonate of soda to remove smells from fabric and carpets rather than masking them with chemical scents.
51		Conduct a meeting online over Skype or Zoom instead of travelling.
52		Replace cleaning products with more environmentally friendly versions or even make your own. This is better for the environment, and can reduce indoor pollution in your home.
53		Donate old clothes to charity or take them to a fabric recycling point. Old shoes can also be donated or recycled.
54		Change the way you shave! Switch to using a safety razor, brush and shaving soap this week. A good safety razor will last you a lifetime. There are lots of websites to get you started if you have not used one before, and have tips to help you make it a moment of luxury in your day rather than a chore. Disposable razors are made from a mixture of metal and plastic that cannot easily be disassembled for recycling, ending up in landfill. The brush and soap will replace aerosol cans and plastic pumps too.

No	✓	Challenge
55		This week find out about and try to reduce the impact of microfibers. Around 60% of the clothes we buy are made from synthetic fibers like nylon and polyester, which are types of plastic. Each time we wash our clothes we wash away thousands of microfibers. These can make their way to the sea contributing to microplastic pollution, being eaten by sea creatures and becoming part of the ocean food chain. Check the labels when buying new clothes and try to choose natural fibres where possible, also get into the routine of washing your clothes when they need it, not just out of the habit of throwing it in the laundry bin at the end of the day. This week write, email or social message the manufacturer of your washing machine asking them to research the possibility of fiber filters for washing machines.
56		Next time you are online shopping, or about to hit one click purchase on Amazon, add it to your saved items or wishlist instead and wait three days before checking out. If you still want or need it in three days time, go ahead and buy it.
57		Consider buying environmentally friendly toilet roll in bulk, wrapped in paper and delivered in a cardboard box. Buying like this is often cheaper and reduces packaging waste.
58		Conduct an energy saving audit of your home. Choose one area to improve.
59		Get a greenhouse or polytunnel and extend your growing season.
60		Go litter picking this week, and aim to go once a month. Safety first - remember to use gloves and a picker, avoid broken glass and clinical waste and report any potentially dangerous items you find to your local environmental office.
61		Each time a lightbulb goes from now on replace it with the most eco-friendly version you can afford.
62		Buy a reusable water bottle made of glass or metal and take it with you instead of single use plastic bottles.
63		Help bats in your garden. Plant night scented flowers, put up a bat box for roosting, leave some untidy areas in your garden to help insect life flourish and reduce or remove outside lighting at night.

No	✓	Challenge
64		Knit or crochet dish cleaning cloths. You can do this using cotton yarn, or even old cotton t-shirts.
65		Plant a tree, either on your own land or through a scheme in your local area.
66		Create a bumblebee nest somewhere quiet in your garden using an upturned pot partly buried in the soil filled with some straw or dried leaves inside. Add a section of hosepipe going through the soil from the outside to inside the pot to create an access tunnel for the bees in and out of their new home.
67		Shop locally for one week. Is it possible to get everything you need? Are there some local shops you could continue to visit once the challenge is over?
68		Help local conservation groups by recording wildlife near you. Most areas have a butterfly or moth count, or a garden bird count. Find out what is being run in your area and join in this year. This data helps wildlife conservation charities focus their efforts on the wildlife that is struggling the most.
69		Swap two toiletries or makeup for more environmentally friendly or cruelty free versions this week.
70		Replace paper napkins with cloth ones that can be washed and used again. Look for linen as a more environmentally friendly option, or make your own with fabric remnants.
71		Find your local glass recycling centre and recycle some glass!
72		Make one swap for a fair-trade item this week.
73		Dry clothes outside in good weather.
74		Source reusable glass or plastic boxes to keep cheese and other foods fresh in the fridge instead of single use plastic bags.
75		Research sources of sustainable clothing in styles you like. Look for clothes that last and ditch disposable fashion. Research your options this week making it easier to make a more environmentally friendly choice next time you need to purchase an item of clothing.

No	✓	Challenge
76		Introduce meat free Mondays – or any day of the week that works for you. This means having meat free meals and snacks all day, there are lots of recipe ideas online if you search 'Meat Free Mondays'. It's a great opportunity to try something new each week.
77		Replace throw away items like paper plates, cups, plastic forks and knives with something that can be reused.
78		Make a list of single use plastics that you regularly use and think about which you could phase out, and what you would replace them with. Then make a start and swap at least one out.
79		Check your toiletries for microbeads, could you replace any of them with something more friendly?
80		Don't mow all your grass this week. Allow a few areas to have longer grass which is preferred by beetles, shrews and other wildlife. These grass 'islands' can be an attractive feature as well as significantly increasing the biodiversity in your lawn.
81		Double use water. Water used for washing or peeling veg can go on the garden in summer. Clean recycling items when you have finished washing up your dishes before you throw the water away, rather than running them under the tap.
82		Find out what nature is declining in your area. Is there a way you can help?
83		Add a small wildlife pond to your garden creating a hotspot for biodiversity in your area. Many ponds have been lost in recent years, so even adding a small freshwater habitat can make a big difference where you live. Fill the pond with rainwater, add plants that are native to your local area, and watch the wildlife move in!
84		Plan a weeks' worth of meals with a view to reducing waste. Can ingredients or leftovers from one meal become part of the next? Can you shop so you have everything you need, but not too much? Shopping and cooking in this way can cut down on waste and save you time and money. Create three or four weekly meal plans like this and you can rotate them.
85		While waiting for your shower to warm up put a bucket underneath to catch the water - you can use this to water plants or flush the loo.

No	✓	Challenge
86		Make the most of your local charity and second-hand shops. Have a tidy up - take unused clothes, kitchenware and children's toys to the local charity shops, jumble sales and similar. Be a regular visitor and supporter and buy 'pre-loved' where you can.
87		Get your next item of clothing or homeware from a second-hand shop, or buy used from eBay, local Facebook groups or other local reselling groups. Re use the many things we already have circulating in society.
88		Visit a farmer's market or smaller local vegetable van or farm, or try out a delivered fruit and vegetable box instead of buying from the supermarket this week.
89		Check your regular beauty buys to see if they are cruelty free - if not research alternatives for when you have to replace them next.
90		Make a bug hotel for your garden using twigs, logs, old bamboo canes, leaves and other natural materials. Providing a rich environment for insect life helps other wildlife to flourish including birds and amphibians.
91		Upcycle something instead of throwing it away.
92		Think about the things that you buy this week, where and how they were made. Is there a better or fairer alternative? Become more aware of the origins of the things that you buy and the people that produced them and consider fair trade especially for items like bananas, cocoa, sugar, rice and spices.
93		This week look at the products you use to launder your clothes. Laundry liquids that contain bleach, phosphates, chemical fragrances, dyes, phthalates and parabens can cause problems when they get in natural waterways. There are lots of ecologically friendly makes on the market, or you can even try a laundry ball or soap nuts as alternative ways to clean your clothes. These options are also more friendly to sensitive skin.
94		Clean three things in your home using either lemon juice, vinegar or bicarbonate of soda. How did it work out?
95		Become palm oil aware. Check the labels of things you buy this week, if the palm oil in a product has been grown in a sustainable way it will have the RSPO label, or be marked as RSPO or sustainable in the ingredients list. Is it possible to swap for a sustainable choice?

No	✓	Challenge
96		Join or start a car share for work.
97		Invest in some cotton or jute tote bags and bring them shopping with you every time. Put a slim foldable bag in with your purse or coat pocket so it is always there.
98		Work on reducing your food waste this week. Log everything you bin for one week and ask yourself how it compares to a typical week. If you bin 5 soggy bananas each week, can you change your shopping habits so you throw less away? Can you make better use of the freezer to store food that might otherwise go over?
99		A lot of wrapping paper is made with plastic meaning it cannot be recycled. Buy recyclable wrapping paper, or consider wrapping gifts alternatively, in reusable bags, with cloth like the Japanese do, or in baskets or boxes.
100		Buy seafood that is sustainable. Research sustainable fish or download the app - swap one unsustainable fish you use regularly for a sustainable one (For example, you might swap Cod for MSC certified Alaskan pollock)
101		This week make sure to turn lights off when leaving a room.

My Challenges

Write in your own ideas for challenges.

✓	Challenge

My Challenges

✓	Challenge

My Challenges

✓	Challenge

My Challenges

✓	Challenge

Weekly Tracker

Week Beginning:

○ *Monday*

○ *Tuesday*

○ *Wednesday*

○ *Thursday*

○ *Friday*

○ *Saturday*

○ *Sunday*

This week's challenge.

How did it go?

Rate this challenge.

☆ ☆ ☆ ☆ ☆

Will you keep it up?

Weekly Habit Tracker	M	T	W	T	F	S	S

How I made a difference this week.

How I felt this week.

My biggest take away from this week.

Biggest win this week.

Week Beginning:

- [ ] *Monday*
- [ ] *Tuesday*
- [ ] *Wednesday*
- [ ] *Thursday*
- [ ] *Friday*
- [ ] *Saturday*
- [ ] *Sunday*

This week's challenge.

How did it go?

Rate this challenge.

☆ ☆ ☆ ☆ ☆

Will you keep it up?

Weekly Habit Tracker	M	T	W	T	F	S	S

How I made a difference this week.

How I felt this week.

My biggest take away from this week.

Biggest win this week.

Week Beginning:

○ *Monday*

○ *Tuesday*

○ *Wednesday*

○ *Thursday*

○ *Friday*

○ *Saturday*

○ *Sunday*

This week's challenge.

How did it go?

Rate this challenge.

☆ ☆ ☆ ☆ ☆

Will you keep it up?

Weekly Habit Tracker	M	T	W	T	F	S	S

How I made a difference this week.

How I felt this week.

My biggest take away from this week.

Biggest win this week.

Week Beginning:

- ○ *Monday*
- ○ *Tuesday*
- ○ *Wednesday*
- ○ *Thursday*
- ○ *Friday*
- ○ *Saturday*
- ○ *Sunday*

This week's challenge.

How did it go?

Rate this challenge.

☆ ☆ ☆ ☆ ☆

Will you keep it up?

Weekly Habit Tracker	M	T	W	T	F	S	S

How I made a difference this week.

How I felt this week.

My biggest take away from this week.

Biggest win this week.

Four Weekly Check-In

Out of the last four challenges which will you bring forward with you?

Challenge 1	Challenge 2	Challenge 3	Challenge 4

How did it go overall in the last four weeks?

What was the biggest challenge you faced?

What was your most positive moment?

Four Weekly Check-In

Do you have any ideas for future challenges or changes to this challenge?

Have you made a difference in the last four weeks, however small?

Name a way you can reward yourself for your progress so far:

Go to page 152 and color in a reward stamp for each week you completed!

Week Beginning:

○ *Monday*

○ *Tuesday*

○ *Wednesday*

○ *Thursday*

○ *Friday*

○ *Saturday*

○ *Sunday*

This week's challenge.

How did it go?

Rate this challenge.

☆ ☆ ☆ ☆ ☆

Will you keep it up?

Weekly Habit Tracker	M	T	W	T	F	S	S

How I made a difference this week.

How I felt this week.

My biggest take away from this week.

Biggest win this week.

Week Beginning:

○ *Monday*

○ *Tuesday*

○ *Wednesday*

○ *Thursday*

○ *Friday*

○ *Saturday*

○ *Sunday*

This week's challenge.

How did it go?

Rate this challenge.

☆ ☆ ☆ ☆ ☆

Will you keep it up?

Weekly Habit Tracker	M	T	W	T	F	S	S

How I made a difference this week.

How I felt this week.

My biggest take away from this week.

Biggest win this week.

Week Beginning:

Monday

Tuesday

Wednesday

Thursday

Friday

Saturday

Sunday

This week's challenge.

How did it go?

Rate this challenge.

☆ ☆ ☆ ☆ ☆

Will you keep it up?

Weekly Habit Tracker	M	T	W	T	F	S	S

How I made a difference this week.

How I felt this week.

My biggest take away from this week.

Biggest win this week.

Week Beginning:

○ *Monday*

○ *Tuesday*

○ *Wednesday*

○ *Thursday*

○ *Friday*

○ *Saturday*

○ *Sunday*

This week's challenge.

How did it go?

Rate this challenge.

☆ ☆ ☆ ☆ ☆

Will you keep it up?

Weekly Habit Tracker	M	T	W	T	F	S	S

How I made a difference this week.

How I felt this week.

My biggest take away from this week.

Biggest win this week.

Out of the last four challenges which will you bring forward with you?

Challenge 1	Challenge 2	Challenge 3	Challenge 4

How did it go overall in the last four weeks?

What was the biggest challenge you faced?

What was your most positive moment?

Do you have any ideas for future challenges or changes to this challenge?

Have you made a difference in the last four weeks, however small?

Name a way you can reward yourself for your progress so far:

Go to page 152 and color in a reward stamp for each week you completed!

Week Beginning:

○ *Monday*

○ *Tuesday*

○ *Wednesday*

○ *Thursday*

○ *Friday*

○ *Saturday*

○ *Sunday*

This week's challenge.

How did it go?

Rate this challenge.

☆ ☆ ☆ ☆ ☆

Will you keep it up?

Weekly Habit Tracker	M	T	W	T	F	S	S

How I made a difference this week.

How I felt this week.

My biggest take away from this week.

Biggest win this week.

Week Beginning:

- ○ *Monday*
- ○ *Tuesday*
- ○ *Wednesday*
- ○ *Thursday*
- ○ *Friday*
- ○ *Saturday*
- ○ *Sunday*

This week's challenge.

How did it go?

Rate this challenge.

☆ ☆ ☆ ☆ ☆

Will you keep it up?

Weekly Habit Tracker	M	T	W	T	F	S	S

How I made a difference this week.

How I felt this week.

My biggest take away from this week.

Biggest win this week.

Week Beginning:

○ *Monday*

○ *Tuesday*

○ *Wednesday*

○ *Thursday*

○ *Friday*

○ *Saturday*

○ *Sunday*

This week's challenge.

How did it go?

Rate this challenge.

☆ ☆ ☆ ☆ ☆

Will you keep it up?

Weekly Habit Tracker	M	T	W	T	F	S	S

How I made a difference this week.

How I felt this week.

My biggest take away from this week.

Biggest win this week.

Week Beginning:

○ *Monday*

○ *Tuesday*

○ *Wednesday*

○ *Thursday*

○ *Friday*

○ *Saturday*

○ *Sunday*

This week's challenge.

How did it go?

Rate this challenge.

☆ ☆ ☆ ☆ ☆

Will you keep it up?

Weekly Habit Tracker	M	T	W	T	F	S	S

How I made a difference this week.

How I felt this week.

My biggest take away from this week.

Biggest win this week.

Four Weekly Check-In

Out of the last four challenges which will you bring forward with you?

Challenge 1	Challenge 2	Challenge 3	Challenge 4

How did it go overall in the last four weeks?

What was the biggest challenge you faced?

What was your most positive moment?

Four Weekly Check-In

Do you have any ideas for future challenges or changes to this challenge?

Have you made a difference in the last four weeks, however small?

Name a way you can reward yourself for your progress so far:

Go to page 152 and color in a reward stamp for each week you completed!

Week Beginning:

Monday

Tuesday

Wednesday

Thursday

Friday

Saturday

Sunday

This week's challenge.

How did it go?

Rate this challenge.

☆ ☆ ☆ ☆ ☆

Will you keep it up?

Weekly Habit Tracker	M	T	W	T	F	S	S

How I made a difference this week.

How I felt this week.

My biggest take away from this week.

Biggest win this week.

Week Beginning:

○ *Monday*

○ *Tuesday*

○ *Wednesday*

○ *Thursday*

○ *Friday*

○ *Saturday*

○ *Sunday*

This week's challenge.

How did it go?

Rate this challenge.

☆ ☆ ☆ ☆ ☆

Will you keep it up?

Weekly Habit Tracker	M	T	W	T	F	S	S

How I made a difference this week.

How I felt this week.

My biggest take away from this week.

Biggest win this week.

Week Beginning:

Monday

Tuesday

Wednesday

Thursday

Friday

Saturday

Sunday

This week's challenge.

How did it go?

Rate this challenge.

☆ ☆ ☆ ☆ ☆

Will you keep it up?

Weekly Habit Tracker	M	T	W	T	F	S	S

How I made a difference this week.

How I felt this week.

My biggest take away from this week.

Biggest win this week.

Week Beginning:

○ *Monday*

○ *Tuesday*

○ *Wednesday*

○ *Thursday*

○ *Friday*

○ *Saturday*

○ *Sunday*

This week's challenge.

How did it go?

Rate this challenge.

☆ ☆ ☆ ☆ ☆

Will you keep it up?

Weekly Habit Tracker	M	T	W	T	F	S	S

How I made a difference this week.

How I felt this week.

My biggest take away from this week.

Biggest win this week.

Four Weekly Check-In

Out of the last four challenges which will you bring forward with you?

Challenge 1	Challenge 2	Challenge 3	Challenge 4

How did it go overall in the last four weeks?

What was the biggest challenge you faced?

What was your most positive moment?

Do you have any ideas for future challenges or changes to this challenge?

Have you made a difference in the last four weeks, however small?

Name a way you can reward yourself for your progress so far:

Go to page 152 and color in a reward stamp for each week you completed!

Week Beginning:

○ *Monday*

○ *Tuesday*

○ *Wednesday*

○ *Thursday*

○ *Friday*

○ *Saturday*

○ *Sunday*

This week's challenge.

How did it go?

Rate this challenge.

☆ ☆ ☆ ☆ ☆

Will you keep it up?

Weekly Habit Tracker	M	T	W	T	F	S	S

How I made a difference this week.

How I felt this week.

My biggest take away from this week.

Biggest win this week.

Week Beginning:

○ *Monday*

○ *Tuesday*

○ *Wednesday*

○ *Thursday*

○ *Friday*

○ *Saturday*

○ *Sunday*

This week's challenge.

How did it go?

Rate this challenge.

☆ ☆ ☆ ☆ ☆

Will you keep it up?

Weekly Habit Tracker	M	T	W	T	F	S	S

How I made a difference this week.

How I felt this week.

My biggest take away from this week.

Biggest win this week.

Week Beginning:

- ○ *Monday*
- ○ *Tuesday*
- ○ *Wednesday*
- ○ *Thursday*
- ○ *Friday*
- ○ *Saturday*
- ○ *Sunday*

This week's challenge.

How did it go?

Rate this challenge.

☆ ☆ ☆ ☆ ☆

Will you keep it up?

Weekly Habit Tracker	M	T	W	T	F	S	S

How I made a difference this week.

How I felt this week.

My biggest take away from this week.

Biggest win this week.

Week Beginning:

- ○ *Monday*
- ○ *Tuesday*
- ○ *Wednesday*
- ○ *Thursday*
- ○ *Friday*
- ○ *Saturday*
- ○ *Sunday*

This week's challenge.

How did it go?

Rate this challenge.

☆ ☆ ☆ ☆ ☆

Will you keep it up?

Weekly Habit Tracker	M	T	W	T	F	S	S

How I made a difference this week.

How I felt this week.

My biggest take away from this week.

Biggest win this week.

Four Weekly Check-In

Out of the last four challenges which will you bring forward with you?

Challenge 1	Challenge 2	Challenge 3	Challenge 4

How did it go overall in the last four weeks?

What was the biggest challenge you faced?

What was your most positive moment?

Four Weekly Check-In

Do you have any ideas for future challenges or changes to this challenge?

Have you made a difference in the last four weeks, however small?

Name a way you can reward yourself for your progress so far:

Go to page 152 and color in a reward stamp for each week you completed!

Week Beginning:

○ *Monday*

○ *Tuesday*

○ *Wednesday*

○ *Thursday*

○ *Friday*

○ *Saturday*

○ *Sunday*

This week's challenge.

How did it go?

Rate this challenge.

☆ ☆ ☆ ☆ ☆

Will you keep it up?

Weekly Habit Tracker	M	T	W	T	F	S	S

How I made a difference this week.

How I felt this week.

My biggest take away from this week.

Biggest win this week.

Week Beginning:

- ○ *Monday*
- ○ *Tuesday*
- ○ *Wednesday*
- ○ *Thursday*
- ○ *Friday*
- ○ *Saturday*
- ○ *Sunday*

This week's challenge.

How did it go?

Rate this challenge.

☆ ☆ ☆ ☆ ☆

Will you keep it up?

Weekly Habit Tracker	M	T	W	T	F	S	S

How I made a difference this week.

How I felt this week.

My biggest take away from this week.

Biggest win this week.

Week Beginning:

○ *Monday*

○ *Tuesday*

○ *Wednesday*

○ *Thursday*

○ *Friday*

○ *Saturday*

○ *Sunday*

This week's challenge.

How did it go?

Rate this challenge.

☆ ☆ ☆ ☆ ☆

Will you keep it up?

Weekly Habit Tracker	M	T	W	T	F	S	S

How I made a difference this week.

How I felt this week.

My biggest take away from this week.

Biggest win this week.

Week Beginning:

○ *Monday*

○ *Tuesday*

○ *Wednesday*

○ *Thursday*

○ *Friday*

○ *Saturday*

○ *Sunday*

This week's challenge.

How did it go?

Rate this challenge.

☆ ☆ ☆ ☆ ☆

Will you keep it up?

Weekly Habit Tracker	M	T	W	T	F	S	S

How I made a difference this week.

How I felt this week.

My biggest take away from this week.

Biggest win this week.

Four Weekly Check-In

Out of the last four challenges which will you bring forward with you?

Challenge 1	Challenge 2	Challenge 3	Challenge 4

How did it go overall in the last four weeks?

What was the biggest challenge you faced?

What was your most positive moment?

Do you have any ideas for future challenges or changes to this challenge?

Have you made a difference in the last four weeks, however small?

Name a way you can reward yourself for your progress so far:

Go to page 152 and color in a reward stamp for each week you completed!

Week Beginning:

○ *Monday*

○ *Tuesday*

○ *Wednesday*

○ *Thursday*

○ *Friday*

○ *Saturday*

○ *Sunday*

This week's challenge.

How did it go?

Rate this challenge.

☆ ☆ ☆ ☆ ☆

Will you keep it up?

Weekly Habit Tracker	M	T	W	T	F	S	S

How I made a difference this week.

How I felt this week.

My biggest take away from this week.

Biggest win this week.

Week Beginning:

- ○ *Monday*
- ○ *Tuesday*
- ○ *Wednesday*
- ○ *Thursday*
- ○ *Friday*
- ○ *Saturday*
- ○ *Sunday*

This week's challenge.

How did it go?

Rate this challenge.

☆ ☆ ☆ ☆ ☆

Will you keep it up?

Weekly Habit Tracker	M	T	W	T	F	S	S

How I made a difference this week.

How I felt this week.

My biggest take away from this week.

Biggest win this week.

Week Beginning:

- ○ *Monday*
- ○ *Tuesday*
- ○ *Wednesday*
- ○ *Thursday*
- ○ *Friday*
- ○ *Saturday*
- ○ *Sunday*

This week's challenge.

How did it go?

Rate this challenge.

☆ ☆ ☆ ☆ ☆

Will you keep it up?

Weekly Habit Tracker	M	T	W	T	F	S	S

How I made a difference this week.

How I felt this week.

My biggest take away from this week.

Biggest win this week.

Week Beginning:

- ○ *Monday*
- ○ *Tuesday*
- ○ *Wednesday*
- ○ *Thursday*
- ○ *Friday*
- ○ *Saturday*
- ○ *Sunday*

This week's challenge.

How did it go?

Rate this challenge.

☆ ☆ ☆ ☆ ☆

Will you keep it up?

Weekly Habit Tracker	M	T	W	T	F	S	S

How I made a difference this week.

How I felt this week.

My biggest take away from this week.

Biggest win this week.

Out of the last four challenges which will you bring forward with you?

Challenge 1	Challenge 2	Challenge 3	Challenge 4

How did it go overall in the last four weeks?

What was the biggest challenge you faced?

What was your most positive moment?

Do you have any ideas for future challenges or changes to this challenge?

Have you made a difference in the last four weeks, however small?

Name a way you can reward yourself for your progress so far:

Go to page 152 and color in a reward stamp for each week you completed!

Week Beginning:

○ *Monday*

○ *Tuesday*

○ *Wednesday*

○ *Thursday*

○ *Friday*

○ *Saturday*

○ *Sunday*

This week's challenge.

How did it go?

Rate this challenge.

☆ ☆ ☆ ☆ ☆

Will you keep it up?

Weekly Habit Tracker	M	T	W	T	F	S	S

How I made a difference this week.

How I felt this week.

My biggest take away from this week.

Biggest win this week.

Week Beginning:

○ *Monday*

○ *Tuesday*

○ *Wednesday*

○ *Thursday*

○ *Friday*

○ *Saturday*

○ *Sunday*

This week's challenge.

How did it go?

Rate this challenge.

☆ ☆ ☆ ☆ ☆

Will you keep it up?

Weekly Habit Tracker	M	T	W	T	F	S	S

How I made a difference this week.

How I felt this week.

My biggest take away from this week.

Biggest win this week.

Week Beginning:

- ○ *Monday*
- ○ *Tuesday*
- ○ *Wednesday*
- ○ *Thursday*
- ○ *Friday*
- ○ *Saturday*
- ○ *Sunday*

This week's challenge.

How did it go?

Rate this challenge.

☆ ☆ ☆ ☆ ☆

Will you keep it up?

Weekly Habit Tracker	M	T	W	T	F	S	S

How I made a difference this week.

How I felt this week.

My biggest take away from this week.

Biggest win this week.

Week Beginning:

○ *Monday*

○ *Tuesday*

○ *Wednesday*

○ *Thursday*

○ *Friday*

○ *Saturday*

○ *Sunday*

This week's challenge.

How did it go?

Rate this challenge.

☆ ☆ ☆ ☆ ☆

Will you keep it up?

Weekly Habit Tracker	M	T	W	T	F	S	S

How I made a difference this week.

How I felt this week.

My biggest take away from this week.

Biggest win this week.

Out of the last four challenges which will you bring forward with you?

Challenge 1	Challenge 2	Challenge 3	Challenge 4

How did it go overall in the last four weeks?

What was the biggest challenge you faced?

What was your most positive moment?

Do you have any ideas for future challenges or changes to this challenge?

Have you made a difference in the last four weeks, however small?

Name a way you can reward yourself for your progress so far:

Go to page 152 and color in a reward stamp for each week you completed!

Week Beginning:

○ *Monday*

○ *Tuesday*

○ *Wednesday*

○ *Thursday*

○ *Friday*

○ *Saturday*

○ *Sunday*

This week's challenge.

How did it go?

Rate this challenge.

☆ ☆ ☆ ☆ ☆

Will you keep it up?

Weekly Habit Tracker	M	T	W	T	F	S	S

How I made a difference this week.

How I felt this week.

My biggest take away from this week.

Biggest win this week.

Week Beginning:

○ *Monday*

○ *Tuesday*

○ *Wednesday*

○ *Thursday*

○ *Friday*

○ *Saturday*

○ *Sunday*

This week's challenge.

How did it go?

Rate this challenge.

☆ ☆ ☆ ☆ ☆

Will you keep it up?

Weekly Habit Tracker	M	T	W	T	F	S	S

How I made a difference this week.

How I felt this week.

My biggest take away from this week.

Biggest win this week.

Week Beginning:

○ *Monday*

○ *Tuesday*

○ *Wednesday*

○ *Thursday*

○ *Friday*

○ *Saturday*

○ *Sunday*

This week's challenge.

How did it go?

Rate this challenge.

☆ ☆ ☆ ☆ ☆

Will you keep it up?

Weekly Habit Tracker	M	T	W	T	F	S	S

How I made a difference this week.

How I felt this week.

My biggest take away from this week.

Biggest win this week.

Week Beginning:

- ◯ *Monday*
- ◯ *Tuesday*
- ◯ *Wednesday*
- ◯ *Thursday*
- ◯ *Friday*
- ◯ *Saturday*
- ◯ *Sunday*

This week's challenge.

How did it go?

Rate this challenge.

☆ ☆ ☆ ☆ ☆

Will you keep it up?

Weekly Habit Tracker	M	T	W	T	F	S	S

How I made a difference this week.

How I felt this week.

My biggest take away from this week.

Biggest win this week.

Four Weekly Check-In

Out of the last four challenges which will you bring forward with you?

Challenge 1	Challenge 2	Challenge 3	Challenge 4

How did it go overall in the last four weeks?

What was the biggest challenge you faced?

What was your most positive moment?

Four Weekly Check-In

Do you have any ideas for future challenges or changes to this challenge?

Have you made a difference in the last four weeks, however small?

Name a way you can reward yourself for your progress so far:

Go to page 152 and color in a reward stamp for each week you completed!

Week Beginning:

○ *Monday*

○ *Tuesday*

○ *Wednesday*

○ *Thursday*

○ *Friday*

○ *Saturday*

○ *Sunday*

This week's challenge.

How did it go?

Rate this challenge.

☆ ☆ ☆ ☆ ☆

Will you keep it up?

Weekly Habit Tracker	M	T	W	T	F	S	S

How I made a difference this week.

How I felt this week.

My biggest take away from this week.

Biggest win this week.

Week Beginning:

○ *Monday*

○ *Tuesday*

○ *Wednesday*

○ *Thursday*

○ *Friday*

○ *Saturday*

○ *Sunday*

This week's challenge.

How did it go?

Rate this challenge.

☆ ☆ ☆ ☆ ☆

Will you keep it up?

Weekly Habit Tracker	M	T	W	T	F	S	S

How I made a difference this week.

How I felt this week.

My biggest take away from this week.

Biggest win this week.

Week Beginning:

○ *Monday*

○ *Tuesday*

○ *Wednesday*

○ *Thursday*

○ *Friday*

○ *Saturday*

○ *Sunday*

This week's challenge.

How did it go?

Rate this challenge.

☆ ☆ ☆ ☆ ☆

Will you keep it up?

Weekly Habit Tracker	M	T	W	T	F	S	S

How I made a difference this week.

How I felt this week.

My biggest take away from this week.

Biggest win this week.

Week Beginning:

○ *Monday*

○ *Tuesday*

○ *Wednesday*

○ *Thursday*

○ *Friday*

○ *Saturday*

○ *Sunday*

This week's challenge.

How did it go?

Rate this challenge.

☆ ☆ ☆ ☆ ☆

Will you keep it up?

Weekly Habit Tracker	M	T	W	T	F	S	S

How I made a difference this week.

How I felt this week.

My biggest take away from this week.

Biggest win this week.

Four Weekly Check-In

Out of the last four challenges which will you bring forward with you?

Challenge 1	Challenge 2	Challenge 3	Challenge 4

How did it go overall in the last four weeks?

What was the biggest challenge you faced?

What was your most positive moment?

Do you have any ideas for future challenges or changes to this challenge?

Have you made a difference in the last four weeks, however small?

Name a way you can reward yourself for your progress so far:

Go to page 152 and color in a reward stamp for each week you completed!

Week Beginning:

○ *Monday*

○ *Tuesday*

○ *Wednesday*

○ *Thursday*

○ *Friday*

○ *Saturday*

○ *Sunday*

This week's challenge.

How did it go?

Rate this challenge.

☆ ☆ ☆ ☆ ☆

Will you keep it up?

Weekly Habit Tracker	M	T	W	T	F	S	S

How I made a difference this week.

How I felt this week.

My biggest take away from this week.

Biggest win this week.

Week Beginning:

○ *Monday*

○ *Tuesday*

○ *Wednesday*

○ *Thursday*

○ *Friday*

○ *Saturday*

○ *Sunday*

This week's challenge.

How did it go?

Rate this challenge.

☆ ☆ ☆ ☆ ☆

Will you keep it up?

Weekly Habit Tracker	M	T	W	T	F	S	S

How I made a difference this week.

How I felt this week.

My biggest take away from this week.

Biggest win this week.

Week Beginning:

○ *Monday*

○ *Tuesday*

○ *Wednesday*

○ *Thursday*

○ *Friday*

○ *Saturday*

○ *Sunday*

This week's challenge.

How did it go?

Rate this challenge.

☆ ☆ ☆ ☆ ☆

Will you keep it up?

Weekly Habit Tracker	M	T	W	T	F	S	S

How I made a difference this week.

How I felt this week.

My biggest take away from this week.

Biggest win this week.

Week Beginning:

- ○ *Monday*
- ○ *Tuesday*
- ○ *Wednesday*
- ○ *Thursday*
- ○ *Friday*
- ○ *Saturday*
- ○ *Sunday*

This week's challenge.

How did it go?

Rate this challenge.

☆ ☆ ☆ ☆ ☆

Will you keep it up?

Weekly Habit Tracker	M	T	W	T	F	S	S

How I made a difference this week.

How I felt this week.

My biggest take away from this week.

Biggest win this week.

Out of the last four challenges which will you bring forward with you?

Challenge 1	Challenge 2	Challenge 3	Challenge 4

How did it go overall in the last four weeks?

What was the biggest challenge you faced?

What was your most positive moment?

Do you have any ideas for future challenges or changes to this challenge?

Have you made a difference in the last four weeks, however small?

Name a way you can reward yourself for your progress so far:

Go to page 152 and color in a reward stamp for each week you completed!

Week Beginning:

○ *Monday*

○ *Tuesday*

○ *Wednesday*

○ *Thursday*

○ *Friday*

○ *Saturday*

○ *Sunday*

This week's challenge.

How did it go?

Rate this challenge.

☆ ☆ ☆ ☆ ☆

Will you keep it up?

Weekly Habit Tracker	M	T	W	T	F	S	S

How I made a difference this week.

How I felt this week.

My biggest take away from this week.

Biggest win this week.

Week Beginning:

○ *Monday*

○ *Tuesday*

○ *Wednesday*

○ *Thursday*

○ *Friday*

○ *Saturday*

○ *Sunday*

This week's challenge.

How did it go?

Rate this challenge.

☆ ☆ ☆ ☆ ☆

Will you keep it up?

Weekly Habit Tracker	M	T	W	T	F	S	S

How I made a difference this week.

How I felt this week.

My biggest take away from this week.

Biggest win this week.

Week Beginning:

○ *Monday*

○ *Tuesday*

○ *Wednesday*

○ *Thursday*

○ *Friday*

○ *Saturday*

○ *Sunday*

This week's challenge.

How did it go?

Rate this challenge.

☆ ☆ ☆ ☆ ☆

Will you keep it up?

Weekly Habit Tracker	M	T	W	T	F	S	S

How I made a difference this week.

How I felt this week.

My biggest take away from this week.

Biggest win this week.

Week Beginning:

○ *Monday*

○ *Tuesday*

○ *Wednesday*

○ *Thursday*

○ *Friday*

○ *Saturday*

○ *Sunday*

This week's challenge.

How did it go?

Rate this challenge.

☆ ☆ ☆ ☆ ☆

Will you keep it up?

Weekly Habit Tracker	M	T	W	T	F	S	S

How I made a difference this week.

How I felt this week.

My biggest take away from this week.

Biggest win this week.

Four Weekly Check-In

Out of the last four challenges which will you bring forward with you?

Challenge 1	Challenge 2	Challenge 3	Challenge 4

How did it go overall in the last four weeks?

What was the biggest challenge you faced?

What was your most positive moment?

Do you have any ideas for future challenges or changes to this challenge?

Have you made a difference in the last four weeks, however small?

Name a way you can reward yourself for your progress so far:

Go to page 152 and color in a reward stamp for each week you completed!

Week Beginning:

- ○ *Monday*
- ○ *Tuesday*
- ○ *Wednesday*
- ○ *Thursday*
- ○ *Friday*
- ○ *Saturday*
- ○ *Sunday*

This week's challenge.

How did it go?

Rate this challenge.

☆ ☆ ☆ ☆ ☆

Will you keep it up?

Weekly Habit Tracker	M	T	W	T	F	S	S

How I made a difference this week.

How I felt this week.

My biggest take away from this week.

Biggest win this week.

Week Beginning:

- ○ *Monday*
- ○ *Tuesday*
- ○ *Wednesday*
- ○ *Thursday*
- ○ *Friday*
- ○ *Saturday*
- ○ *Sunday*

This week's challenge.

How did it go?

Rate this challenge.

☆ ☆ ☆ ☆ ☆

Will you keep it up?

Weekly Habit Tracker	M	T	W	T	F	S	S

How I made a difference this week.

How I felt this week.

My biggest take away from this week.

Biggest win this week.

Week Beginning:

○ *Monday*

○ *Tuesday*

○ *Wednesday*

○ *Thursday*

○ *Friday*

○ *Saturday*

○ *Sunday*

This week's challenge.

How did it go?

Rate this challenge.

☆ ☆ ☆ ☆ ☆

Will you keep it up?

Weekly Habit Tracker	M	T	W	T	F	S	S

How I made a difference this week.

How I felt this week.

My biggest take away from this week.

Biggest win this week.

Week Beginning:

○ *Monday*

○ *Tuesday*

○ *Wednesday*

○ *Thursday*

○ *Friday*

○ *Saturday*

○ *Sunday*

This week's challenge.

How did it go?

Rate this challenge.

☆ ☆ ☆ ☆ ☆

Will you keep it up?

Weekly Habit Tracker	M	T	W	T	F	S	S

How I made a difference this week.

How I felt this week.

My biggest take away from this week.

Biggest win this week.

Congratulations, you did it!

You should be incredibly proud, you have completed 52 environmentally friendly weekly challenges. That's a huge achievement! Take some time to reflect on how it has gone, the contribution you have made, and what you will take forwards with you.

Go back through the list of challenges at the beginning of the book. Using a different colour pen tick all the challenges that you have kept up.

What are you doing as natural now that you weren't doing at the beginning of this challenge?

What would you recommend to friends and family?

Do you feel your contribution has made a difference to the environment and your life?

Think about your contribution over the whole year if you added it up, what would it look like? Many fewer plastic items used? Electricity saved? What would it look like if you kept these changes up for another year? or another five years?

Now cook yourself a special meal, go for a walk in a beautiful place, or find another way to pat yourself on the back for an amazing year!

Color in a reward stamp for each week you complete!

29
30
31
32
33
34
35
36
37
38
39
40
41
42
43
44
45
46
47
48
49
50
51
52

Made in United States
Orlando, FL
30 April 2025

60888418R00090